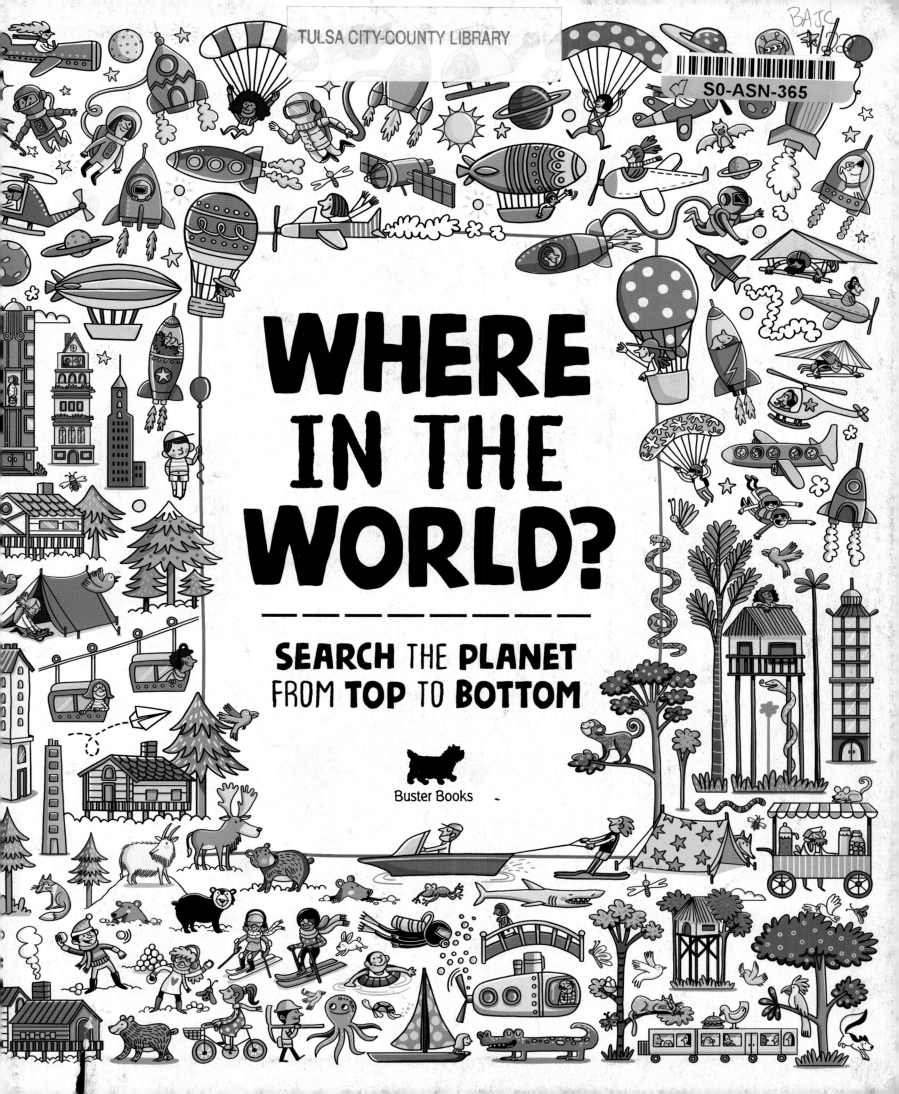

WHERE IN THE WORLD?

SEARCH THE PLANET FROM TOP TO BOTTOM

Buster Books

Illustrated by
Paula Bossio

Written and edited by Susannah Bailey
Designed by Zoe Bradley
Cover design by Angie Allison

First published in Great Britain in 2021 by Buster Books,
an imprint of Michael O'Mara Books Limited, 9 Lion Yard,
Tremadoc Road, London SW4 7NQ

W www.mombooks.com/buster   f Buster Books   🐦 @BusterBooks

Text and illustrations copyright © Buster Books 2021

A CIP catalogue record for this book is available from the British Library.

Hardback ISBN: 978-1-78055-753-3
Paperback ISBN: 978-1-78055-733-5

1 3 5 7 9 10 8 6 4 2

This book was printed in December 2020 by Leo Paper Products Ltd, Heshan Astros Printing Limited,
Xuantan Temple Industrial Zone, Gulao Town, Heshan City, Guangdong Province, China.

LET THE ADVENTURE BEGIN

Where in the world can you spot an astronaut, a skyscraper or a shark? To find out, you must take an amazing journey through this book. Your tour will start in the starry heights of space, then you will dive down past Earth's snowy mountains and busy cities until you reach the depths of the sea.

As you go down through each level there are people, animals and objects to search for. Can you see a skydiver hurtling through the sky? Or find a frog leaping between two tall trees? Or spot a fireman putting out an underground fire?

Along the way discover fascinating facts about the world's record breakers – the speediest, tallest, heaviest things around you.

There are over 150 things to look out for – will you be able to discover where in the world they are?

UP IN SPACE

You begin in outer space – a faraway place packed with astronauts, rockets and planets.

CAN YOU FIND ...?

1. An **astronaut** carrying a **red flag**.
2. A **rocket** with a **star** on it.
3. A **satellite** with bright **yellow wings**.
4. A **moon** orbiting a **blue and green planet**.
5. **Six** shooting **stars**.
6. A **planet** with a **purple ring** around it.
7. A swirling **black hole**.
8. An **astronaut** fixing a **spacecraft** with a **tool**.
9. A **space telescope** observing a **red planet**.
10. Two **asteroids** (space rocks) **colliding** with each other.

SPOT THESE BONUS THINGS, TOO:

A. An alien **B.** An astrodog **C.** A pizza slice

The hottest planet in our solar system is Venus. Its temperature can reach 471 degrees Celsius (880 degrees Fahrenheit) – hot enough to melt lead.

Did you know that more than 500,000 bits of space junk (disused, man-made objects) orbit the Earth?

The largest known asteroid is about 530 kilometres (329 miles) in diameter.

The biggest planet in our solar system is Jupiter – it's at least twice as big as all the other planets combined.

Shooting stars can travel at 468,318 kilometres per hour (291,000 miles per hour).

When the world's biggest passenger plane, the Airbus A380, is fully loaded, it can weigh around 574 tonnes (633 tons). That is more than the weight of four blue whales.

HELLO

A magician holds the record for the most magic tricks performed during a single skydive. He completed 11 of them!

Some jet planes can fly faster than the speed of sound. They are called 'supersonic' aircraft.

The furthest a paper plane has ever flown is over 69 metres (226 feet).

Did you know that the first hot-air balloon flight took off in 1783? Its passengers were a sheep, a duck and a rooster.

UP IN THE SKY

Now explore the sky above the Earth's surface. You'll find soaring hot-air balloons, planes and helicopters here.

CAN YOU FIND ...?

1. A **passenger** in a **stripy hot-air balloon**.
2. A **pilot** wearing a **white scarf**.
3. A **skywriter** drawing a **heart**.
4. A **skydiver** who is **screaming** in excitement.
5. Two **rescue workers** dangling from the same **rope**.
6. A **helicopter** with a **blue star** on it.
7. A **paraglider** under a **spotty canopy**.
8. A **girl** in a **plane window** wearing **sunglasses**.
9. A **man** with a **brown beard** and a **red helmet**.
10. A **woman** looking through a pair of **binoculars**.

SPOT THESE BONUS THINGS, TOO:

A. A kite **B.** A star-shaped cloud **C.** A balloon

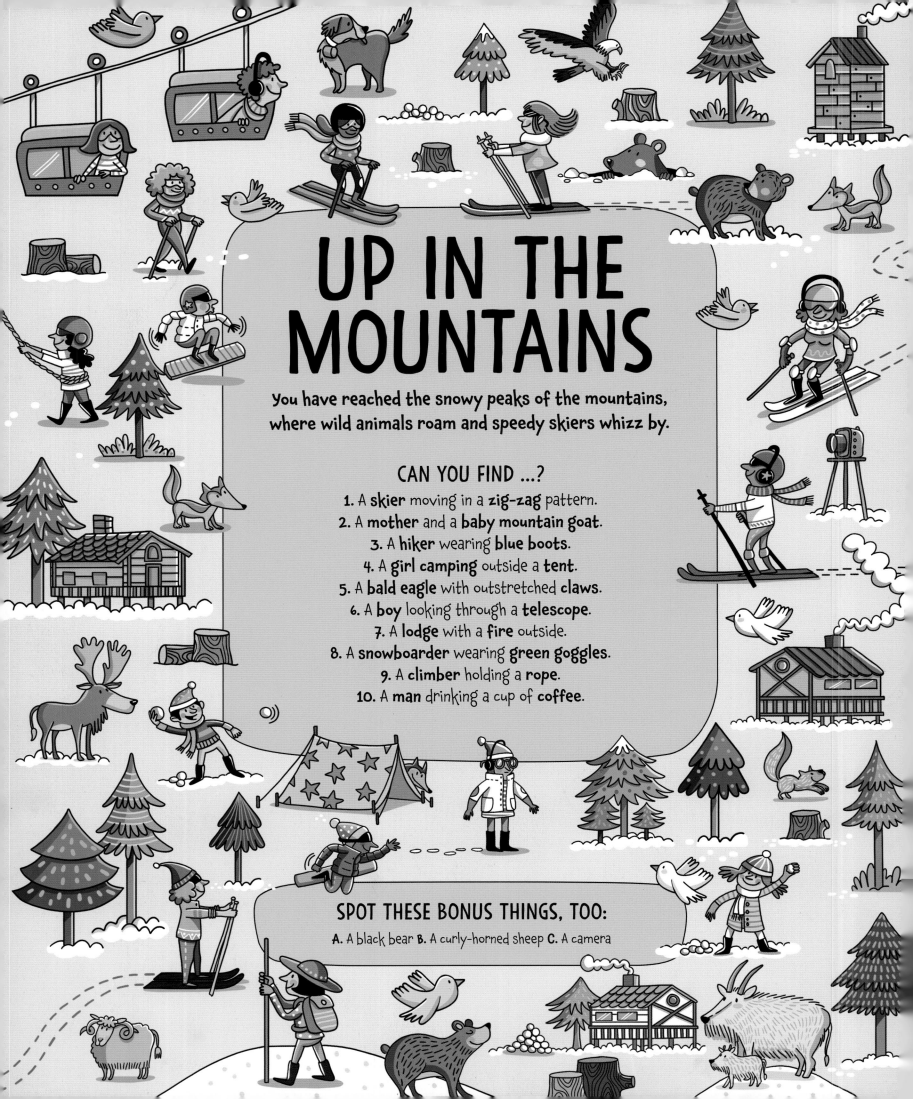

UP IN THE MOUNTAINS

You have reached the snowy peaks of the mountains, where wild animals roam and speedy skiers whizz by.

CAN YOU FIND ...?

1. A **skier** moving in a **zig-zag** pattern.
2. A **mother** and a **baby mountain goat**.
3. A **hiker** wearing **blue boots**.
4. A **girl camping** outside a **tent**.
5. A **bald eagle** with outstretched **claws**.
6. A **boy** looking through a **telescope**.
7. A **lodge** with a **fire** outside.
8. A **snowboarder** wearing **green goggles**.
9. A **climber** holding a **rope**.
10. A **man** drinking a cup of **coffee**.

SPOT THESE BONUS THINGS, TOO:

A. A black bear **B.** A curly-horned sheep **C.** A camera

IN THE TREES

Next is a treetop world, full of swinging monkeys, chirping birds and even a few houses.

CAN YOU FIND ...?

1. A **baby sloth** sleeping on its **mother**.
2. A **pair** of **parrots** chatting to each other.
3. A **bearded** man in a **treehouse**.
4. A **monkey** eating a **banana**.
5. A **bear** climbing up a **tree**.
6. A **bird's nest** with **four eggs** in it.
7. **Five snakes** curled around **tree trunks**.
8. A **red-haired girl** on a treetop **walkway**.
9. A **toucan** with a **blue and red beak**.
10. A **frog** leaping between **two trees**.

SPOT THESE BONUS THINGS, TOO:

A. An upside-down bat **B.** A blue butterfly **C.** A bee

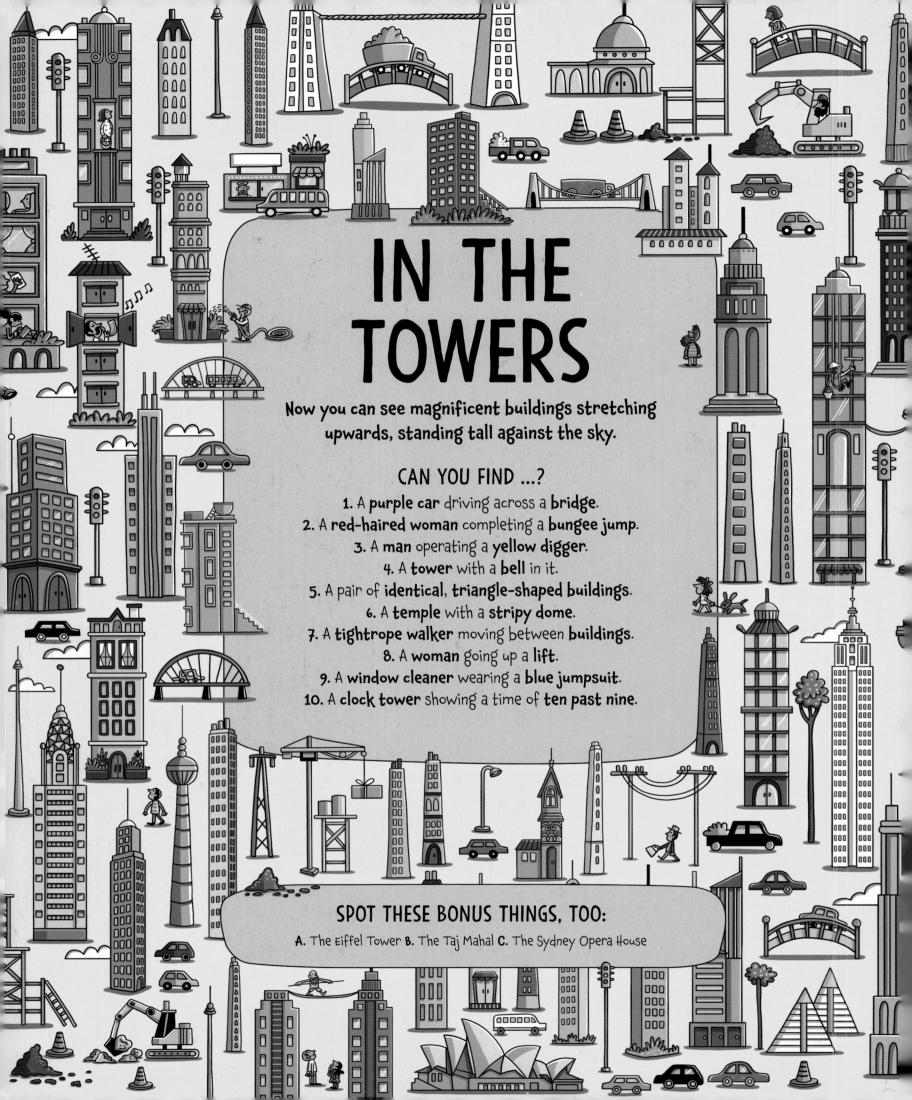

IN THE TOWERS

Now you can see magnificent buildings stretching upwards, standing tall against the sky.

CAN YOU FIND ...?

1. A **purple car** driving across a **bridge**.
2. A **red-haired woman** completing a **bungee jump**.
3. A **man** operating a **yellow digger**.
4. A **tower** with a **bell** in it.
5. A pair of **identical, triangle-shaped buildings**.
6. A **temple** with a **stripy dome**.
7. A **tightrope walker** moving between **buildings**.
8. A **woman** going up a **lift**.
9. A **window cleaner** wearing a **blue jumpsuit**.
10. A **clock tower** showing a time of **ten past nine**.

SPOT THESE BONUS THINGS, TOO:

A. The Eiffel Tower **B.** The Taj Mahal **C.** The Sydney Opera House

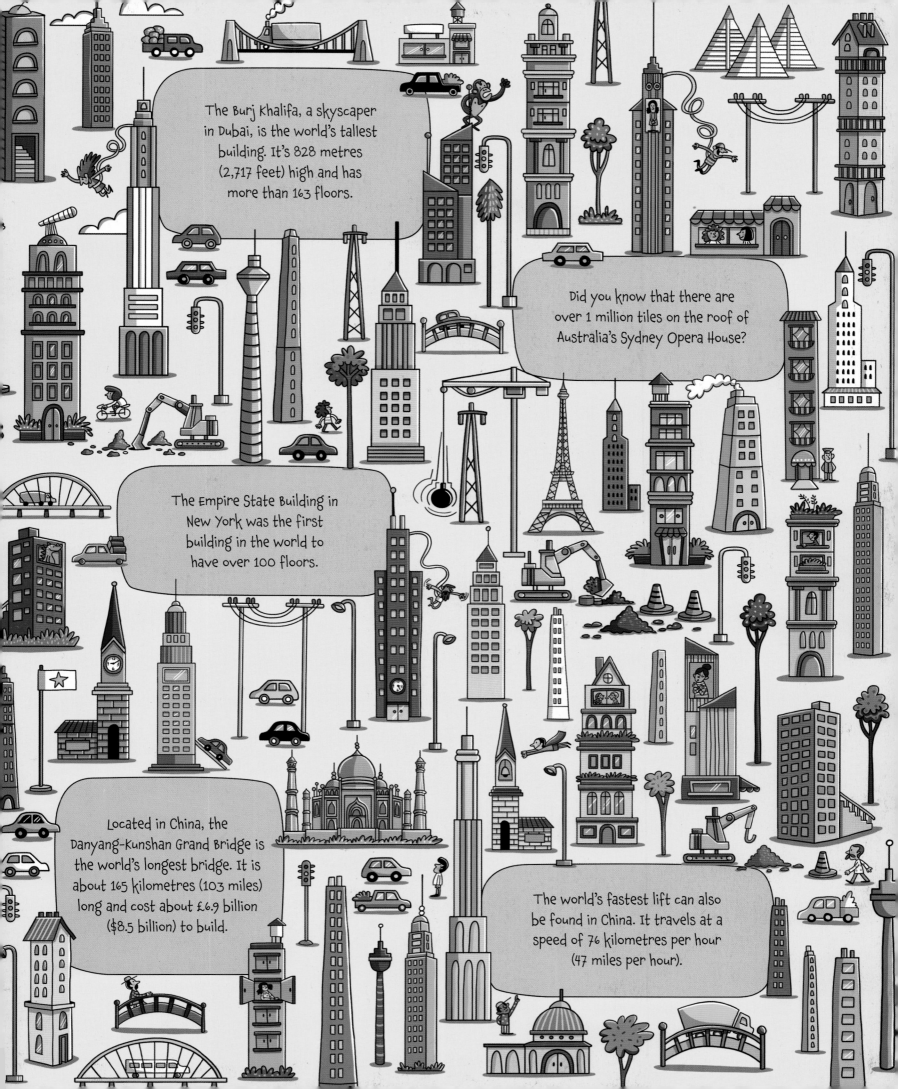

The Burj Khalifa, a skyscaper in Dubai, is the world's tallest building. It's 828 metres (2,717 feet) high and has more than 163 floors.

Did you know that there are over 1 million tiles on the roof of Australia's Sydney Opera House?

The Empire State Building in New York was the first building in the world to have over 100 floors.

Located in China, the Danyang-Kunshan Grand Bridge is the world's longest bridge. It is about 165 kilometres (103 miles) long and cost about £6.9 billion ($8.5 billion) to build.

The world's fastest lift can also be found in China. It travels at a speed of 76 kilometres per hour (47 miles per hour).

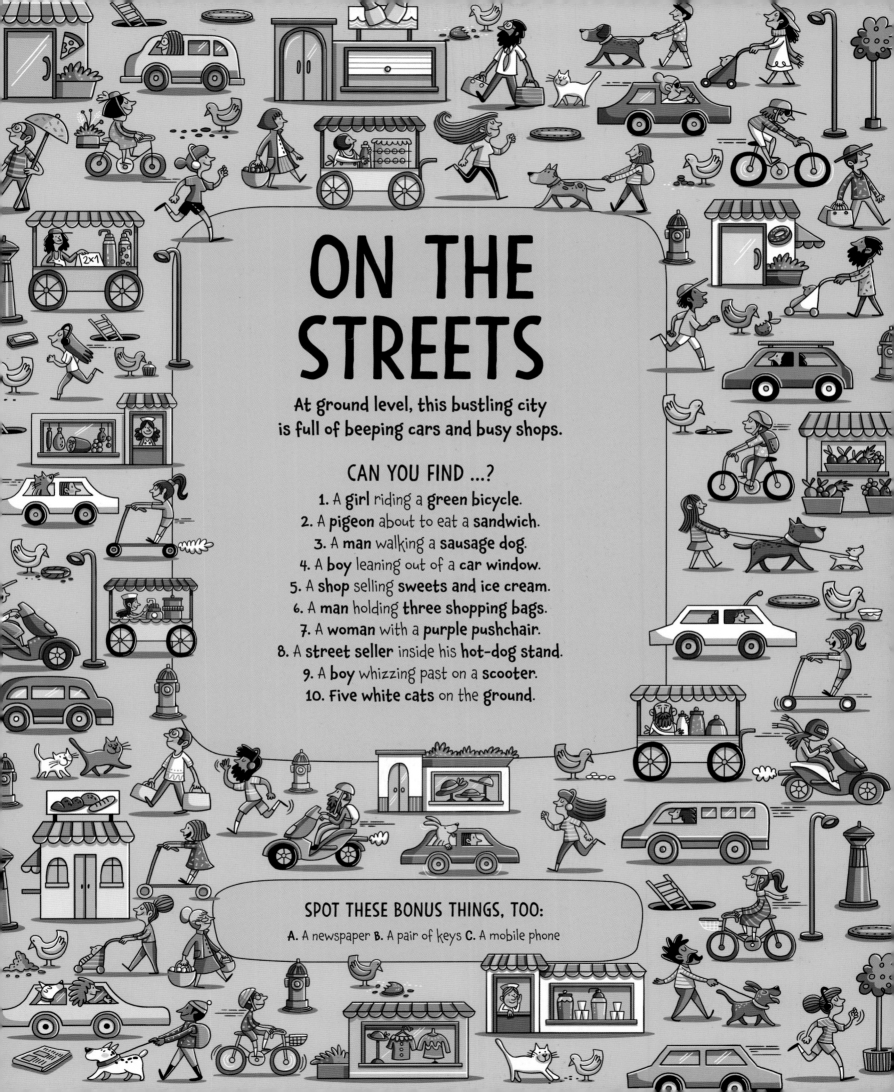

ON THE STREETS

At ground level, this bustling city
is full of beeping cars and busy shops.

CAN YOU FIND ...?

1. A **girl** riding a **green bicycle**.
2. A **pigeon** about to eat a **sandwich**.
3. A **man** walking a **sausage dog**.
4. A **boy** leaning out of a **car window**.
5. A **shop** selling **sweets and ice cream**.
6. A **man** holding **three shopping bags**.
7. A **woman** with a **purple pushchair**.
8. A **street seller** inside his **hot-dog stand**.
9. A **boy** whizzing past on a **scooter**.
10. **Five white cats** on the **ground**.

SPOT THESE BONUS THINGS, TOO:

A. A newspaper **B.** A pair of keys **C.** A mobile phone

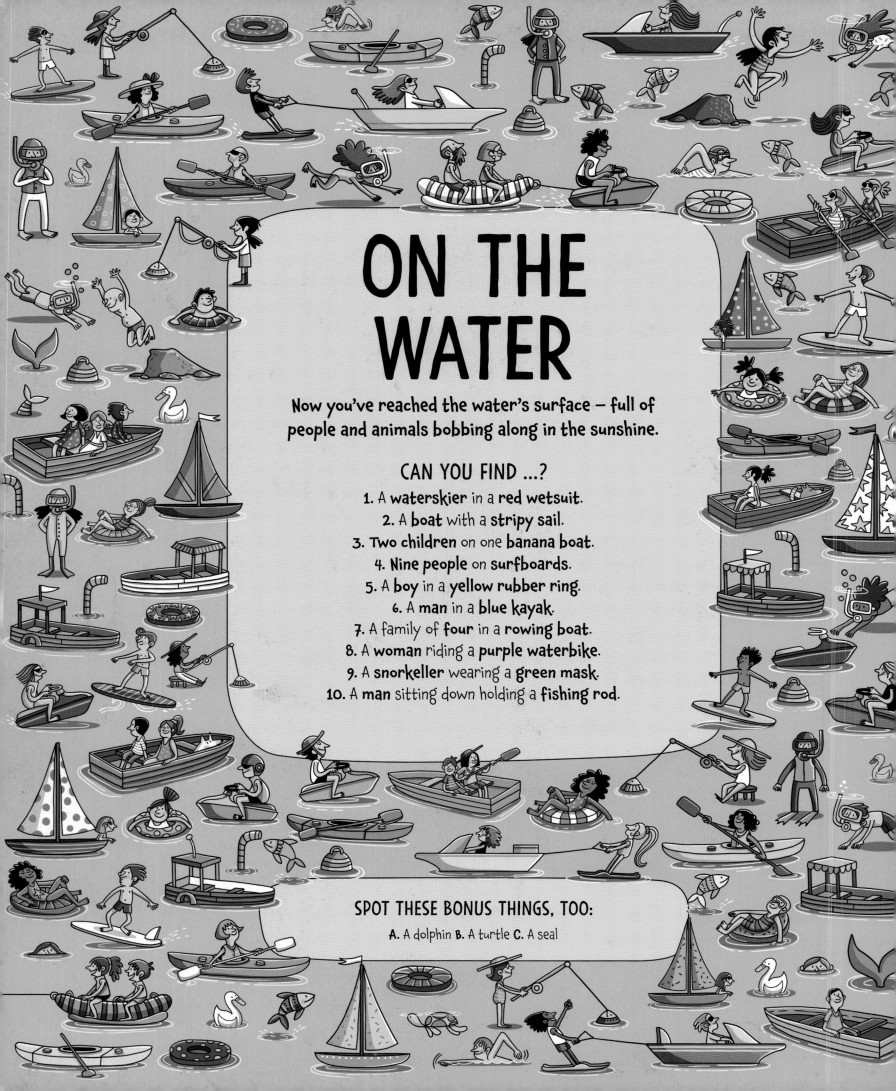

ON THE WATER

Now you've reached the water's surface — full of people and animals bobbing along in the sunshine.

CAN YOU FIND ...?

1. A **waterskier** in a **red wetsuit**.
2. A **boat** with a **stripy sail**.
3. **Two children** on one **banana boat**.
4. **Nine people** on **surfboards**.
5. A **boy** in a **yellow rubber ring**.
6. A **man** in a **blue kayak**.
7. A **family** of **four** in a **rowing boat**.
8. A **woman** riding a **purple waterbike**.
9. A **snorkeller** wearing a **green mask**.
10. A **man** sitting down holding a **fishing rod**.

SPOT THESE BONUS THINGS, TOO:

A. A dolphin **B.** A turtle **C.** A seal

Did you know that about 70 per cent of the Earth's surface is covered by water?

In the longest ever swimming journey, a man swam the entire length of the Amazon River – 5,268 kilometres (3,273 miles). It took him over two months.

The longest ship ever built was the *Seawise Giant*. It was made in Japan and was 458 metres (1,503 feet) long.

There are about 40 species of dolphin in the world. They are found in oceans, rivers and lakes.

The record for the fastest solo journey around the world by boat is held by a sailor who finished the journey in a time of 42 days and 16 hours.

The largest badger sett (underground home) discovered contained a tunnel network roughly 879 metres (2,884 feet) long. It had 178 entrances and 50 underground chambers.

Foxes can give birth to a whopping 11 or 12 babies in one litter. However, the average is more like four or five.

A mole can dig up to 20 metres (66 feet) of tunnel in a single day.

The largest recorded colony of ants is 6,000 kilometres (3,728 miles) long, running from northern Italy to the Atlantic coast of Spain.

Did you know that rabbits can rotate their ears 180 degrees to listen out for predators?

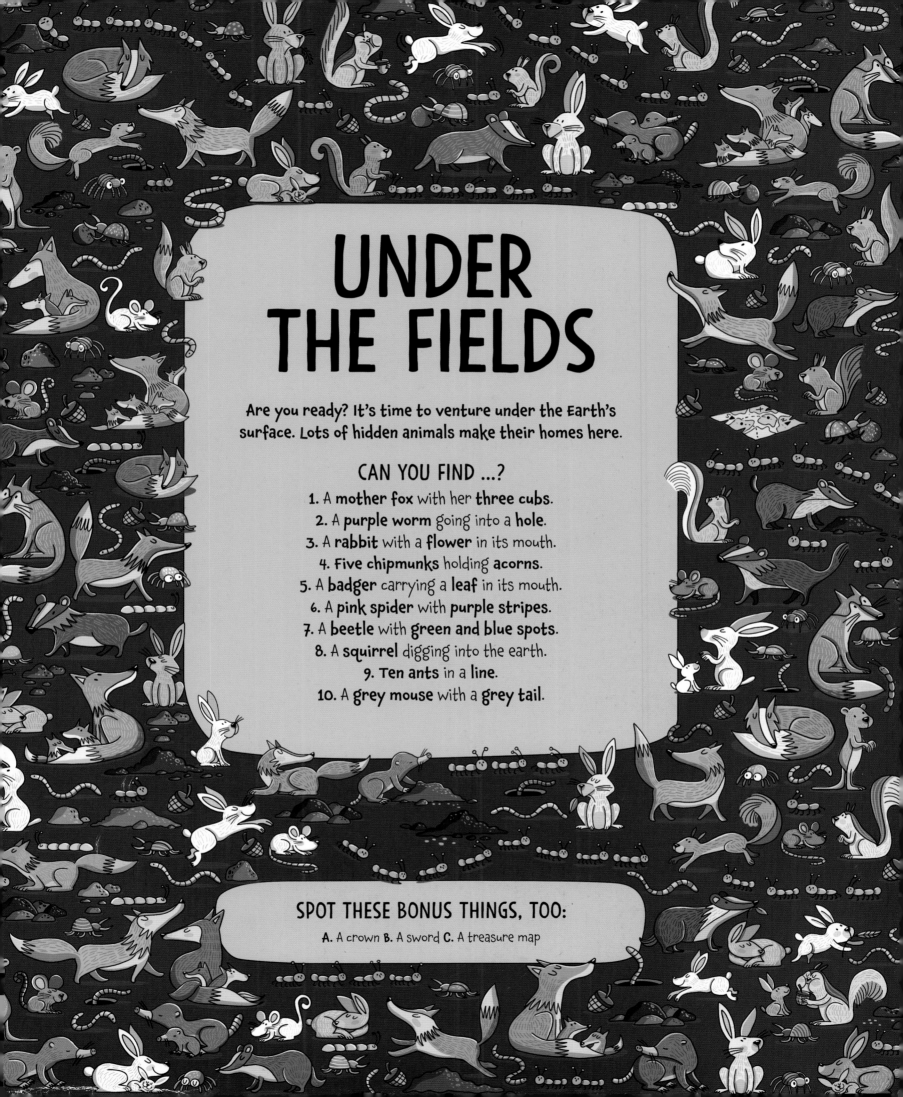

UNDER THE FIELDS

Are you ready? It's time to venture under the Earth's surface. Lots of hidden animals make their homes here.

CAN YOU FIND ...?

1. A **mother fox** with her **three cubs**.
2. A **purple worm** going into a **hole**.
3. A **rabbit** with a **flower** in its mouth.
4. **Five chipmunks** holding **acorns**.
5. A **badger** carrying a **leaf** in its mouth.
6. A **pink spider** with **purple stripes**.
7. A **beetle** with **green and blue spots**.
8. A **squirrel** digging into the earth.
9. **Ten ants** in a **line**.
10. A **grey mouse** with a **grey tail**.

SPOT THESE BONUS THINGS, TOO:

A. A crown **B.** A sword **C.** A treasure map

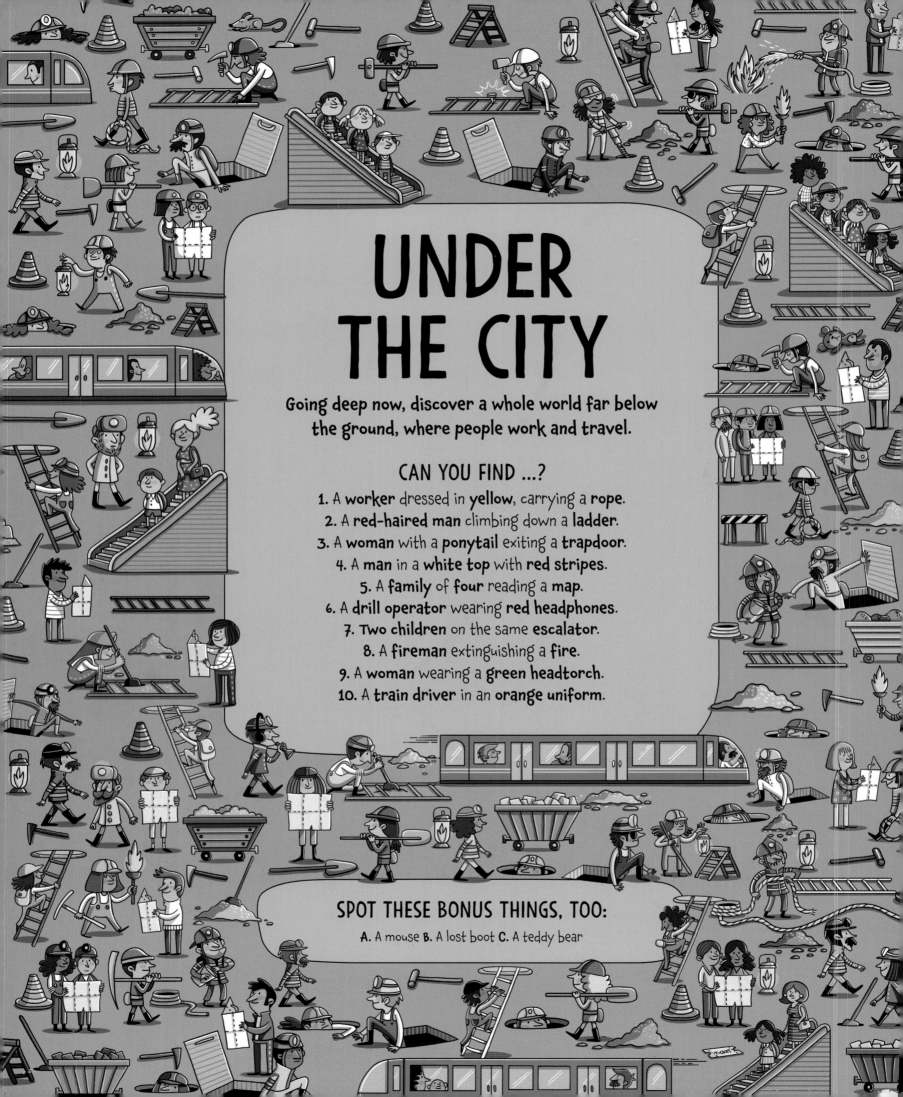

UNDER THE CITY

Going deep now, discover a whole world far below the ground, where people work and travel.

CAN YOU FIND ...?

1. A **worker** dressed in **yellow**, carrying a **rope**.
2. A **red-haired man** climbing down a **ladder**.
3. A **woman** with a **ponytail** exiting a **trapdoor**.
4. A **man** in a **white top** with **red stripes**.
5. A **family** of **four** reading a **map**.
6. A **drill operator** wearing **red headphones**.
7. **Two children** on the same **escalator**.
8. A **fireman** extinguishing a **fire**.
9. A **woman** wearing a **green headtorch**.
10. A **train driver** in an **orange uniform**.

SPOT THESE BONUS THINGS, TOO:

A. A mouse **B.** A lost boot **C.** A teddy bear

Did you know that an underground fire in an American mining town has been burning for over 50 years?

The Earth's deepest man-made hole is the Kola Superdeep Borehole in the Arctic Circle. It is over 12 kilometres (7.5 miles) deep.

Cloaca Maxima (meaning 'great sewer') in Rome is one of the world's oldest sewer systems. It was built by the Romans in the 6th century BCE, and small parts of it are still in use today.

The New York subway has over 400 metro stations — more than any other metro system in the world.

The world's longest railway tunnel, the Gotthard Base Tunnel in Switzerland, is 57 kilometres (35 miles) long.

Jellyfish are amongst the world's oldest creatures. They've been on Earth for hundreds of millions of years, and were around even before the dinosaurs.

There are roughly 32,000 fish species in the world. This is more than all the birds, reptiles, mammals and amphibian species put together.

The Mariana Trench is the deepest place on Earth. At over 11 kilometres (almost 7 miles) deep, Mount Everest could easily fit inside it, with room to spare.

Blue whales are the largest animals to have ever lived on Earth. They can grow over 30 metres (98 feet) long – the length of more than three buses parked end to end.

Did you know that the fearsome great white shark has up to 300 powerful teeth in its mouth?

UNDER THE SEA

Finally, you've reached the furthest down you can travel – the extraordinary depths of the sea.

CAN YOU FIND ...?

1. A scuba diver with yellow flippers.
2. A great white shark showing its sharp teeth.
3. Five jellyfish with purple spots.
4. A stingray with a stripy tail.
5. A crab holding a shell.
6. A pair of pink seahorses.
7. A yellow starfish on a rock.
8. A clownfish swimming out of an anemone.
9. Four red submarines.
10. A blue whale blowing out bubbles.

SPOT THESE BONUS THINGS, TOO:

A. An anchor **B.** A pair of goggles **C.** A mermaid

ALL THE ANSWERS (AND SOME BONUS FACTS)

There are at least a billion trillion stars in the universe. That's more than all the grains of sand on Earth's deserts and beaches combined.

The International Space Station is the largest man-made structure in space. It is 109 metres (357 feet) long and contains bathrooms, places to sleep and even a gym.

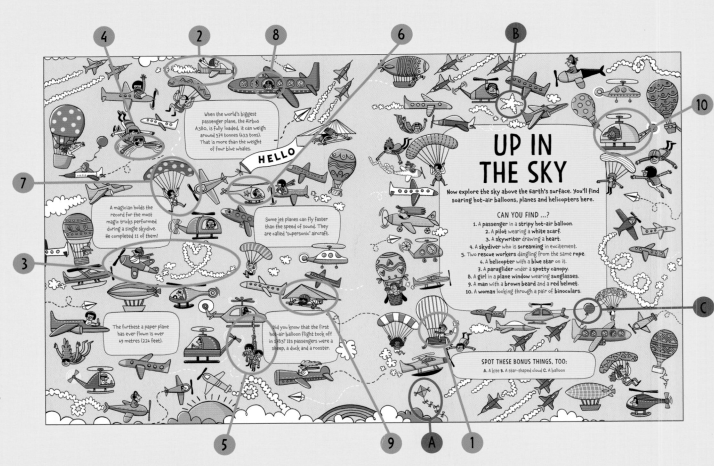

The record for the highest a single kite has ever flown into the sky is 4,880 metres (16,011 feet).

The world's first aeroplane was invented in 1903. Its initial flight lasted for only 12 seconds.

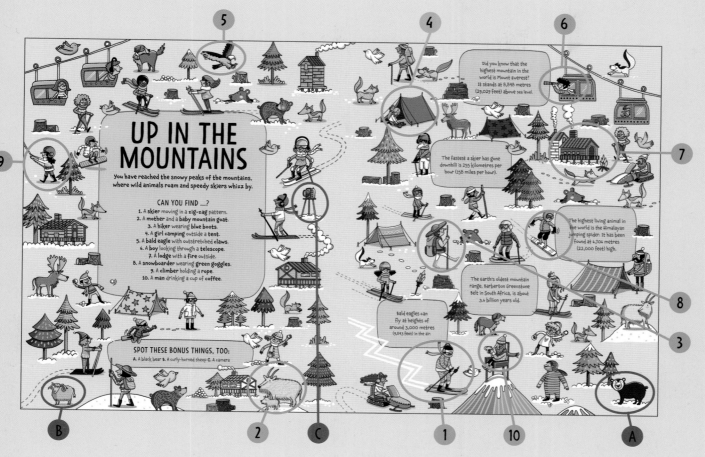

The world's longest mountain range is the Andes, in South America. It is about 8,850 kilometres (5,500 miles) long and crosses seven countries.

Mountain goats are able to jump over 3.5 metres (11.5 feet) in a single leap.

The canopy of leaves in a rainforest is so thick that it can take a raindrop ten minutes to travel from the top of a tree to the ground.

The earliest surviving species of tree, the maidenhair, appeared about 160 million years ago during the Jurassic Period.

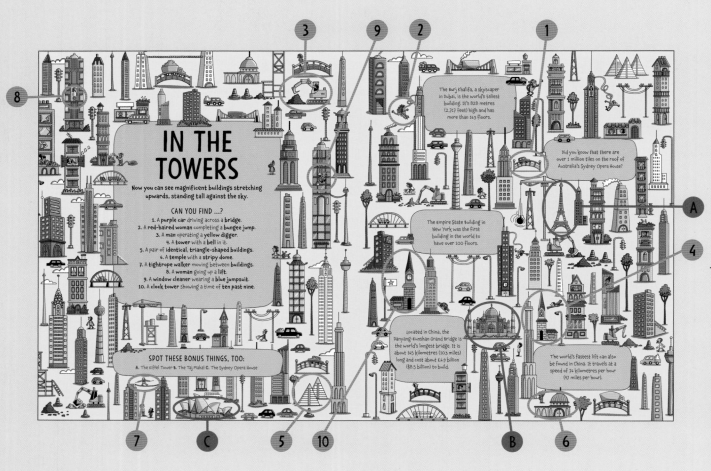

The world's first skyscraper was built in the USA in 1884–1885. It was only ten storeys tall and 42 metres (138 feet) high, but must have seemed gigantic at the time.

The Abraj Al-Bait tower in Mecca, Saudi Arabia, is the world's highest clock tower. At a height of 601 metres (1,972 feet), it is also the third tallest building in the world.

One of Bolivia's capital cities, La Paz, is the highest capital city in the world. It is 3,640 metres (11,942 feet) above sea level.

At 28 metres (92 feet) below sea level, Baku in Azerbaijan is the world's lowest-lying capital city.

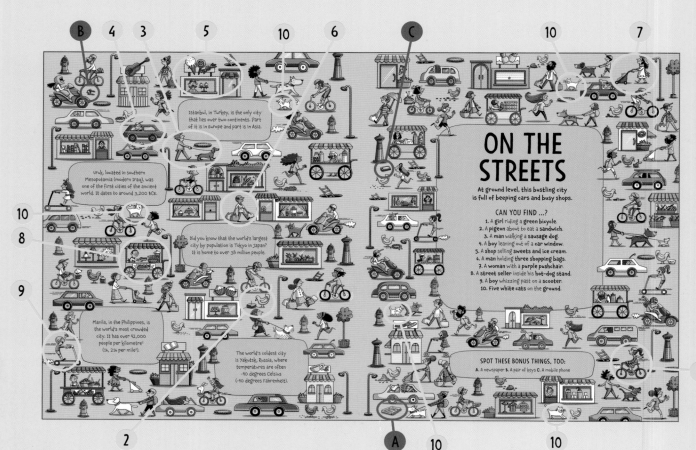

Lake Baikal in Siberia, Russia, holds the world records for the oldest lake, the deepest lake and the largest freshwater lake by volume.

The biggest wave ever surfed was over 24 metres (80 feet) – a world record!

The longest earthworm ever found measured over 6.5 metres (21 feet) when fully extended.

Beetles are the largest group of animals on earth. There are over 350,000 species of them, with many more that are likely to be discovered.

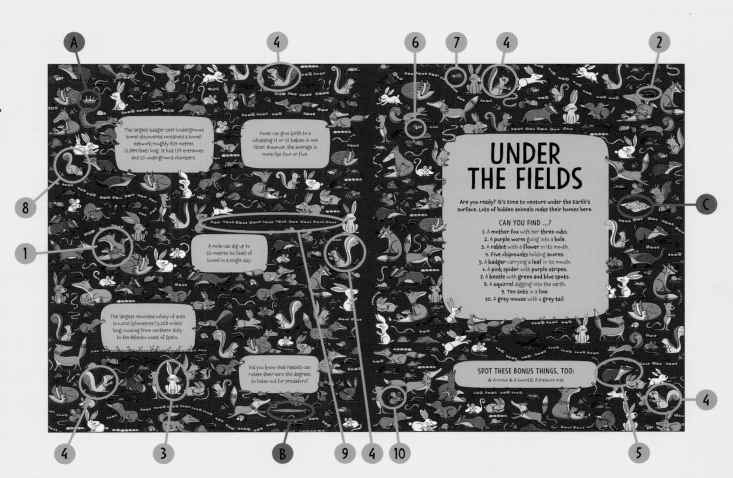

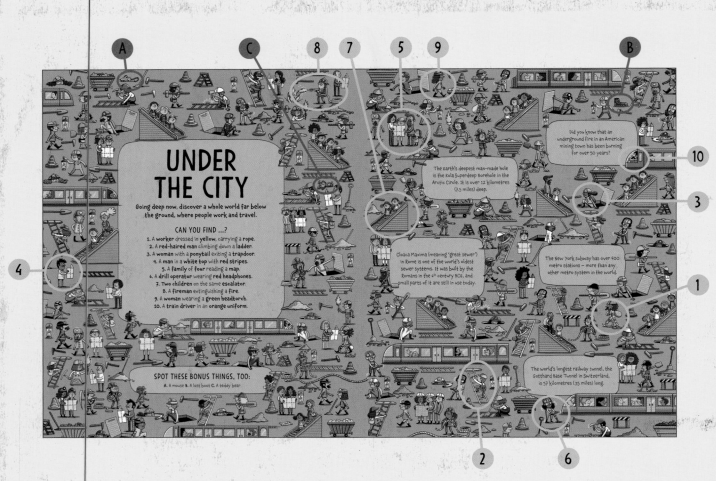

The world's first underground railway was built in London, in the United Kingdom. It started operating underground trains in 1863.

At over 4,000 metres (13,123 feet) under the ground, the Mponeng gold mine in South Africa is the world's deepest mine.

At 1,000 metres (3,821 feet) below sea level, light stops coming through. This is the start of the 'midnight zone', where lots of sea creatures softly glow to create their own light.

The males of only three species get pregnant and give birth to their young, and they all live under the sea. They are the seahorse, the sea dragon and the pipefish.

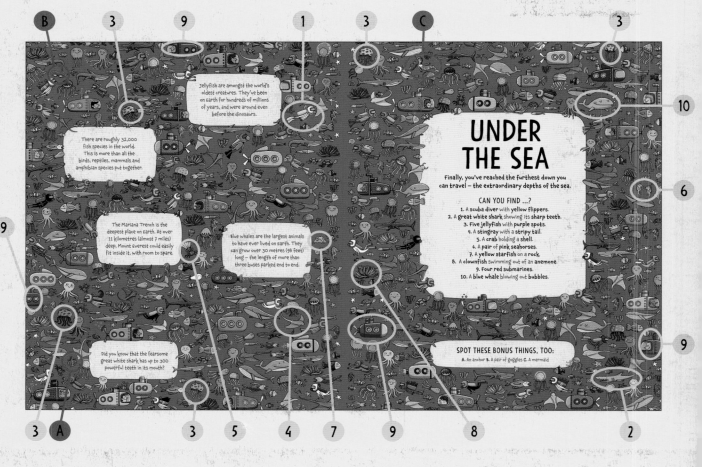